You were the Soul

to my Existence

Also by Amna Dhanani
My Existence Craves Yours

You were the Soul

to my Existence

Amna Dhanani

www.amnadhanani.com
Instagram: **amnadhanani_**
Facebook page: **amnadhanani//**
Twitter: **AmnaDhanani_**

ISBN 978-1-949773-02-6
Ebook ISBN 978-1-949773-03-3

Cover vision by **Amna Dhanani**
Brought to life by **Florencia Musso**
Editing by **S. H. Kazmi**

Acknowledgements

"Not a day goes by
When I don't think about you."
Would be a lie
Because without you
I've been through such a hell
That made me forget even myself.

– Dedicated to the family resting in peace
For playing a part in my growth
When you were here and afterwards too

We miss you
Nani Maan,
Rashi Aunty,
And Bain Aunty.

Contents

When our existences got poured into love
We became one
And as life parted us in two halves
My existence had become my own again
But my soul had left, you.

Pause

Shining Armor

Every evening
I'd go for a walk in the gardens
To get there
I always walked the same stone path
Our meeting was set into one of those stones.
The little kid decided to approach me
After watching me walk alone for weeks
He chose to walk with me in silence every day
This young man with a rare gift called empathy
Chose to stay when others got up and left.
After trying anything and everything
That came to his mind
And after watching
Every mundane move I made
One day
He recognized the storm behind my eyes
And he exclaimed
"I'll be your knight in shining armor!"
For the first time in decades I smiled and said
"Son, you can't rescue me from me."

Quicksand

It's strange
Sometimes how because of one person
You don't want to take a risk with anyone else
Not because you won't be able to trust them
But because you know you will trust them
Yet the fear won't go away
The fear of getting emotionally attached
The fear of things going wrong
Or just not working out
And you getting hurt all over again.
Although this time you'd think
You're prepared,
You can never ready yourself
For a heartbreak.
The effects might be less
And you might know
How to handle it better than you did before
And you might actually heal sooner this time
But in that split second when it happens
And it feels like
Someone made a million tiny little cuts
On your heart
And left it to die a slow death.

And when you don't take the risk
You feel your heart sinking
At the very thought of being surrounded

By the darkness of loneliness
The what ifs
The shattered dreams
A realistic fairytale
Of waking up to someone lying beside you.
It's a quicksand of emotions
That you keep trying to get out of
Needless to say
The more you struggle
The deeper it sucks you in.
It's strange
How one person can mess up your life
For a long time.

Loneliness

How do you begin to speak about loneliness?
How do you know where to start from?
When you see one happy with another
Or when you are all alone at night
When it draws out its claws and attacks you
Or when the panic makes you drown in a crowd
When you're afraid of spending your whole life
In front of a mirror
Having no one to share anything with
Or when you know your nightmare is a truth
You cannot wake up from this reality
Where hopelessness
Doesn't give up a chance to strike
When there's no hand
To pull you out of darkness.
Words aren't enough and will never be
This feeling creates too many holes
That nothing can fill.

What Is Love?

They ask me what is love?
How could I ever describe
What is on the other side of the bridge?
Somewhere I've never been
Because whenever I try to cross it
I get afraid of the heights,
Someone on that side cuts the rope
Or it gets burned down from the middle,
Anyhow I always end up
Where I am standing now.
I can paint a picture from afar
Of what I see but I can't tell you
What fruits that island bears
For I, myself, can only imagine
They hold a special sweetness for me to taste
Because everything on this side
Never nourished my body,
My heart and my soul
As they were supposed to be.

Bittersweet

Out of nowhere a memory of you hit me
And my lips smiled without intention
As a tear rolled down my face
Before I could stop it.

Strange Connection

A piece of me has stuck with you
Since we parted
Little did I know it was my heart
Now it beats in your chest
While I feel pain in mine.
Strange connection we share
I live with no heart
And you live with two
Which belonged to me.

– Since my heart lies in your chest
Tell me, does it hurt?

Stuck

Flowers blooming in the sunlight
Butterflies taking their first flight
Birds singing happiness all around
All the things that express love
Are just a few steps away
Yet my heart is stuck on
The reason because of which
You couldn't stay.

Drained

Your memories have drained
Every drop of blood
Of the idea of love from my heart.

The Weeping

I know that I cried
Over a thousand little things
In front of you
That's why my tears held no value
But when I wept for you
The flowers withered
The moon hid behind the clouds
And the ocean stood still.

Sweet Tears

You were the sweetest thing
That ever happened to me.
I guess that's why
My tears taste sweet as well after you left.

Aflame

You ignited a fire in me
Others couldn't handle
Some ran away in fear
Some stood there and watched me burn.

Inside My Veins

The pain you've given me
Flows inside my veins and makes me forget
About every other pain that exists in my being.

– Every other pain is irrelevant to me

The Melody

Ever since I've recognized love
Everyone knows you as the melody
That dances on the entrance of my heart
While no one is aware
Of a thousand heartbreak songs
You've buried inside of it.

Picture Perfect

You and me
A perfect picture
That was never captured.

*– While everyone talks about how theirs got torn
apart*

You were the Soul to my Existence

Past Tense

I had written poems after poems
Quotes after quotes
A thousand words
A million letters
To reveal how vast the depth
Of my love was for you
All of them written in past tense
To insist it belongs in the past
But you know what
No matter how many walls of proof
I build with my words
The truth is
I still love you and I always will.

– Burned pages

Amna Dhanani

Attached

You have this ability
To make me fall in love
With everything you do.
That is how I fell in love
With the wounds you've given me
Now I've grown too attached with them
To ever let go.

Epiphany

We were wronged by life
For all the right reasons.

Regret

You're that regret
That doesn't feel like one.

Darling Memories

The best part of my day begins at night
With the dark sky
The gossiping stars
The lonely moon
And your darling memories by my side.

Masquerade Ball

The night is too fascinating to sleep
My demons dance with my darkest memories
At midnight
The stars clap
The moon whistles
And the wind whispers in my ears
All the secrets that the darkness keeps.
All night long
They put on masks from an elapsed time
Masks of guests from my past
And they continue dancing
In this vicious masquerade ball
Until the sun comes up
And everything disappears
Like no soul ever existed within these walls.

My Own

Inside my head
I was lost in my own world
I had my own life
You had nothing to do with it
You couldn't touch it
So that's why I stayed within when you left
Even though there was only misery inside me
This was something of my own
Which you weren't.

Amna Dhanani

Mourn

How long do I mourn for something?
That isn't dead but cannot come back.

Cravings

All of my broken pieces crave the pieces
Which don't fit into the puzzle of my life.

Amna Dhanani

Memory Rituals

I'm busy breathing you in
From surroundings
That still have your fragrance
While you're busy washing off
My thoughts with shampoo
As if you rub it hard enough on your scalp
You'll be able to take them out
Like I pull out my hair
When your fragrance burns my nostrils.

Crime Scene

My memories will haunt you
Like the ghost of a victim
Wandering around their crime scene.

Wish Away

I used to keep you awake at nights
Now it's my thought that does.
I'm not something that you can just wish away.

Long Gone

I waited for a long time
For someone who was long gone.

Burn

You're not going to be
A part of my story, my life.
I hope this makes you burn with regret,
A fire that even your tears can't extinguish.

Fragrance of Love

The fragrance you smell around me
You've mistaken it for my love
It's his essence
That he forgot to take with him.

Amna Dhanani

Dead and Alive

I wish I was alive enough to feel your touch
And dead enough to forget his.

Misfortune

I cried for a river
While an ocean was ready to embrace me
That too, with everything
In the darkness of my depths
But how unfortunate
We don't fall for what we need.

Open Door

A cursed heart
At an open door
Forever waiting
For those who never come
And to see those
Who were always there
But only to leave.

The Excuse

I've been using you
As an excuse for my sadness
When in fact
I was lonely before you,
With you
And after you.
At least they'll stop bothering me for now
With all the questions
I don't have the answers to.

Heartbroken

My heart was already broken
Before any man could come into my life
It was broken by the first man I ever saw
My father, who chose to not be in my life.

Color of Love

The color of my father's love was black.
The only time
I saw the red color around him was
When he made my mom's knees bleed.

*– The color red was supposed to be the symbol of
love*

Absence

My mother never let me feel
The absence of my father
I wonder if it was because
I never knew what a father's love is.
Don't get me wrong
What my mother has done for me
Is more than what most mothers would do
Her unconditional love is the reason
I am where I am today
Still at times
I can't help but be curious
What a father's love is?
It has to be different
Than what the world shows me.
I've always had a different perception
About everything around me
But I will never get to learn
More than the pain
He caused my mother and me
Through abandonment,
Hatred and oppression.

Role Model

Silence from every male role model
I've ever had led me to believe that
That's all I can expect from a man
Even though I knew this wasn't true,
Whenever I tried to question that
The society tried to teach me
I'm not supposed to question
Or complain about it
But my only option was to accept it.
That's not why I stayed quiet though
I stopped asking because
I was tired of receiving silence
As an answer too.
So I stopped wasting my energy
And respect on such people altogether.

Sharp Edges

You break me
Then you expect my sharp edges
To not hurt you.

– *They complain I talk back*

Disapproval

They criticize who I've become
After making me the way I am.

Needless Criticism

So many people don't know what they want
But they surely know
How to criticize those who do.

Dreams

When you deny a child to live his dream
You deny a heart to beat.

Amna Dhanani

Acceptance

I won't let myself get consumed
In your disapproval.
What you approve is for your own well being
What I approve is for my own well being
And I accept myself the way I am.

– When your own blood doesn't understand you

Traits

The generation before us
Keeps talking about how our generation
Will never have the same patience
And work as hard as they did
While no one talks about
How the previous generation,
Our own parents lack understanding.
They see our depression as sadness
And our anxiety as an excuse
For not having to work or do house chores.

– *Hypocrisy*

Growing up in a brown family.

Hurt

I learned how to keep getting hurt
By the very people
Who were supposed to teach me
How to love and heal.
I'm not sure if I'm angry
Because of what was done to me
Or sad because they never learned themselves.

Wisdom

If elders have to push their beliefs
Down your throat
Is it really wisdom what they've learned?

Growing up in a brown family.

Norms

You need to understand
What is normal isn't always right.

Sense of Individuality

Don't ever let someone else's opinion
About anything become your own.
Question things, explore within your thoughts
For your own point of view.
While many of us share the same views,
Approaching in your own unique way
Is a way to embrace
Your sense of individuality.

Shackled

Sometimes our hands are shackled by love
Depriving us of the liberty
To do right by ourselves
But the most terrifying part is
The warden can be our parents,
Siblings or significant other.

Perspective

We live in a world where people see
That we are struggling
But not that we are trying.

Burden

If you had to carry what I have to
Even for a mile
You'd forget how to smile.

The Journey of Life

Walk in my shoes for a while
They'll break you
Before you could break them in.

Hardships

There's no doubt in my mind
That everything is going to be okay
For there is ease after hardship.
I'm just afraid
How bad it's going to get before it gets okay.

Steps

I keep pushing myself
And somehow still at times
I find myself behind.

I wonder if that's how life works
Two steps forward
One step behind.

Amna Dhanani

Life

At times
Even a withered tree has more life than me.

Damaged

I inhale love and exhale helplessness.
I wonder what is so damaged in me
That turns hope into suffering.

Storm

Unable to calm the storm in her heart
She used to try and calm the chaos in others
Without realizing that sometimes
Instead of giving her inner peace
It took away what was left of it.

Wounded

My heart bleeds love
I think that's why they keep stabbing it.

Pain vs Love

All the pain combined
That this world has given me
Still isn't as much as my love for him.

Betrayal

I stay away from everyone
Who might say your name
But at night
When I'm trying to put my mind to rest
My own heart betrays me
My heartbeat chants your name.

Amna Dhanani

Your Name

I wonder if it's your name that I carry with me
Or it's the sentence of my death.
It lulls me to sleep every night
As I hold it on my tongue
And your absent presence in my arms
Yet it is your name I wake up screaming
In the middle of the night
And it's what echoes in my empty room
In the morning.
What is it with your name?
That it gives me life and pains me to death.

Victory

Can my heart's voice reach you?
If it cried loud enough
Would it be enough to remind you?
Of all the things we were meant to be together.
I know I'm not seeking some beautiful lie here
I seek the love I know doesn't get lost that easy
Even though we've been through a great deal.

You reminded me of my self-worth
As a human being
As well as a girl in love.
You helped me realize I didn't need anyone
You helped me grow into complete
Just by acknowledging who I was
And how I was.
I'm in pain today but not incomplete without you
And the great tragedy is
I owe this victory to you.

Why Now?

Is it really you? I wonder
Because you're not the type of man
Who looks back and regrets
So tell me why have you returned?
There's nothing left for you to take
And if you've come back to return my love
I don't want something that betrayed me
You can keep it with you as a reminder
Of something real in this fake world.

Thirst

Let me die of thirst
You shouldn't care
When you can't quench it with your love.

Amna Dhanani

An excerpt from
'My Existence Craves Yours'

Snow Globe

I watched you stepping backwards
Through the door
Someone pressed the rewind button
On the dance floor.
All of a sudden it felt like
We never had this dance
Against life
We never even stood a chance.

We came this close
For having it all and then some
Our bodies became one as we waltzed
On the song we used to hum.
What a beautiful sky
And ground covered with snow
Inside the snow globe
We danced slow.

You and I
A perfect groom and bride
Nothing else mattered
Since you were by my side.
What a perfect night
How sad that's all it was

You were the Soul to my Existence

The clock ticked and tocked
So we had to pause.
Since the sun is rising
We'll go back to being dolls
And now on the snow globe
The curtain falls.

But don't despair
As another night will come
The play button will be pressed
And once again we will become one.

– To be continued…

Now Resumed.

Resume

Puppets

We came alive for a lovers' quarrel
Even though we weren't lovers anymore.
We knew how this was going to end
With a new beginning
Attached to an unknown expiration date
But our love had given us life again
How could we decline another chance?
To taste the sweetest thing
This world has to offer
But we could only reincarnate as time's puppets
Our fate played a joke on us again.
So this time we've vowed to stay
Until each stitch is undone into nothing
And we are gone for good at last.
All that will be left
Is this stage with the curtains as our shrouds
Over our skin of threads
And love all around our remains.

Inevitable Torment

I kept asking myself
What was the point of putting myself
Through the inevitable torment again?
I had barely managed to survive last time
But then, when I'm in his arms
And I see all of my pain
Standing on the other side of my world
The silence of my otherwise screaming heart
Asks me, why not?

Stubborn

Even after we parted
I didn't stop making memories with you.
Wherever I went, whatever I did
I knew exactly what you would've said or done.
You were always too predictable
And I was always too stubborn
That is how I never let you leave
Even though I never stopped you.

– You're the life lesson I never learned

Mine

Before the reality hits us
And everything comes crashing down
I'm going to hold you
As if you were always mine
No one else's but mine
Not even yours but only mine.

Relief

I don't remember
When was the last time I was being held
And felt relieved at the same time.

Precious Moments

All I ever wanted was love
And like happiness
I know it's never going to stay
In my life forever
But whatever moments I get with it
I'll make sure I make a life out of them.

Infinity

I never stopped counting the stars
Just as I never stopped loving you.

– Things that only make sense to my heart

Hope

That one star which is brave enough
To shine despite city lights
You're that star for my life.

Tender Love

You are the gentler side of love
I had waited for my whole life.

My Existence Craves Yours

He exists in my life
And that makes all the difference
In my existence.

Beauty and Pain

When I looked into your sad eyes
I was stunned to see how beauty and pain
Can reside at one place at the same time.

Broken Pieces

Your broken pieces are stars to me
The only stars that I can touch.
I'd make love to them
More than I'd make love to you.

Romance

What's more romantic
Than taking care of each other
Without having to speak a single word.

Amna Dhanani

Perfect Fit

You're the right amount of love for me
No more, no less.
You fit perfectly in my heart
Leaving no room for anything which isn't love.

The Right Person

When the right person enters your life
They will never make you feel like
Something is wrong with you
They'll make you realize
Wrong has been done **to you.**

Amna Dhanani

Our Forever

Only in these pages
Our love can become one
With my words being the only sun
Under which we could walk together
With no restrictions
Where the distance
Between you and I isn't so great
Where forever does mean forever.

Reality

The most painful part of reality is
Forever is never forever.

Endless Love

The only reality I want to live in is
Where we love each other endlessly.

Eye-candy

I love it when at the end of the day
I see "I missed you" written all over your face.

Amna Dhanani

Our Love

Every time I kissed you
When you were asleep
You kissed me back
That was your way to say "I love you too."

Insomnia

You are to me
What sleep is to an insomniac.

Amna Dhanani

Remedy

Listening to someone's quiet breathing
Beside you on the bed
Is one of the best natural cures
For all the pain loneliness has ever caused.

Breathing

I breathe in your love
That's how I am still able to breathe.

Amna Dhanani

Underwater

You
Help
Me
Breathe
Underwater.

– Life through chaos

Beauty

I will write your name
On the first ocean wave of dawn
On the heart of a blooming rose
On the smile of a new moon
On the first breeze that welcomes summer
On the last kiss of a purple sunset
On the damp fragrance found after the rain
On the first flight of a white dove
On the blushing autumn leaf
On the bright light of a shooting star
On the spark snow gives to the mountains.
I will write your name
On everything I find beautiful
But still it wouldn't compare
To your morning face.

True Love

The stars twinkle for the sky
Even in the full moon
Until the very last moment before dawn.

– He asked me to define true love

Joy, Peace and Light

Love not only brings joy into our lives
But also peace into our hearts
And light into our souls.

Bee and Flower

My heart splits open for you
To take my love
As if it was only made for you
Which is neither right nor true.

Oblivious

You move me
And my soul at the same time.
I'm not sure if I'm one step closer
To heaven or hell.

Amna Dhanani

A Beautiful Dream

Slowly my life started to feel like
I was waking up from a beautiful dream.
You were still you but different
I was still me but sad.

Not Enough

Every night
You sleep in my arms like
That is all you'd ever want
And then you walk out of this house
Every morning
As if the world is waiting for you to conquer it
As if my heart wasn't enough.

– You needed more, I only needed you

Amna Dhanani

Separation

I knew you needed space
I didn't know you needed it between us.

Prediction

Some people can feel in their bones
Before a storm comes
I can feel in my bones
Before a heartbreak does.

Imminent

Soon all those heartbreaks
They talk about in poetry
Would be mine to feel.

Indifference

The one who cared about me the most
Who treated my scratches
As if they were wounds on his heart
His indifference has given me
A wound which cannot heal.

Invisible

I cry in your arms around me
While you're sound asleep, unaware.
Has my pain become invisible
Or my love has?

Darkness

I stopped fearing darkness
Because you were afraid of it.

– They doubt my love for you

Tragedy

You make love seem like it was made for me
To feel and have but not to keep.

Negligence

You're the only one
Who can understand what I'm going through
And you're the only one
Who chooses not to.

Amna Dhanani

Far Away

You keep me in your arms
Yet I feel as if I'm a million miles away
With the person you used to be.

You and Loneliness

What is it with you and loneliness?
You both come to me at the same time.

Voice of Pain

If you're quiet
Then your eyes speak.
If your eyes are quiet
Then your tears do.

Doubt

Now that my words and my silence
Both don't get to you
I doubt my love ever touched your heart.

Similarity

The only similarity between you and me is
If we both were drowning
I'd save you and you would save yourself too.

Taken For Granted

My heart caught you
Before you had the chance to fall.
Is this why you took me for granted?

Subconsciousness

All the pieces broken by you
I kept hidden from you
And presented you
With the parts of me
That were still whole
In hope that it would fix
What was broken between us
Until there was nothing left to break.

– How I sought love in my subconsciousness

Weak

Our relationship is hanging by a thread
But you've made me so weak
That I can't even tear it apart.

Amna Dhanani

Let go

I'll never get over the fact
That people can change
So much and so suddenly
That they can turn into another person entirely.
One day they could be all about you
And the very next day
You wouldn't be able to recognize
The face of the same person
You've been with for so many years.
The eyes which never lie
Don't show the same feelings for you anymore.
The love and the compassion are gone
As if they were never there.
How do you wrap your head
Around such injustice?
When there's nothing left for you to do
But leave and try to get over
What you hoped would last forever.
Fighting for something that doesn't exist
Sounds like stupidity
Yet that's all you want to do
Because you're ready to put in
Everything you've got but it's no use
Nothing matters anymore
Because it's so freaking gone.
I'll never understand how that happens
I'll never learn how to get over it.

Stop

Amna Dhanani

Heal Me

I went to the river
And demanded the water to cure me
As if it was its responsibility
To heal the wound you gave me.

– Nature heals but it doesn't work that way

Catastrophe

I saved our relationship from everyone
But I couldn't save it from you.

Amna Dhanani

Mourn

I know it's hard to talk about him
And he isn't worth your tears at all
But darling
You need to give his memories
A way out of your system.

Abandonment

The man who had bravely embraced me
With my wounds and scars both
I didn't think one day
He'd be the one to abandon me.
He saved himself
From what he already knew
He was getting into.

Empty House

My heartbeat was his favorite song for a while
And I thought he had found a home in my arms.

– Oh silly me!

Flawed

I had given you the title 'perfect' too soon.
Perfect means forever and more
And you were perfect
Only for a short time.

Player

You told me I was enough
But what we had wasn't
And yet they say I'm the one
Who plays around with words.

Blind

The devotion towards him
Made me unkind towards myself.
I couldn't allow myself to be happy
When he was miserable.
I felt like I was cheating on him
When in fact he was the one
Who cheated me out of my happiness.

Amna Dhanani

The Angelic Monster

You know it would be so easy
To call you the monster
Who broke my heart
And have everyone believe that
Even though it was true,
You don't deserve your name to be
So bitterly remembered.
You always tried to do right by me
Until that was the only thing you did.
It had ended a long time ago
But I was afraid to acknowledge that.

I'm still grateful to you
Despite all that happened between us.
I always knew I deserved better
But when you came along
I didn't know better would be so good.
How can I blame such a person?
Who was so good to me
But how can I not blame the same person?
For not telling me the truth
For letting me hold on to
What didn't even exist anymore.

– *Love*

Your Eyes

It's not your memories that haunt me now
It's your eyes that do.
I've seen them cry for my love
I've seen them longing for the possibility of us
I've seen the determination in them
To do whatever that was in your power
To bring us together forever
Yet it was your eyes
That were so empty like an abyss
So deep, yet no compassion I could find.
The love was gone like it was swallowed up
By the same darkness that lurks under them.
It was your eyes that shot me dead both times.

The Perfect Crime

Breaking my heart was the perfect crime
No one knew
How you slowly killed me with time.

Heartbreaking Performance

My heart breaks
As if it's giving a performance
Taking each piece out of itself so beautifully
Into exact same shape and size.
I wonder to myself
How many times it had to break
To know how to do it so perfectly
As every cell on my body gets awakened in pain
To give my heart a standing ovation
On a marvelous act.

– Goosebumps

The Tears

Here's to the tears
That don't leave my side
By shedding away with the pain
As they were meant to.
They're more loyal to me
Than their partner.
I guess they learned from you
To leave the one who gives you their heart
Or maybe they took a pity
And gave their love to me instead
'Cause you couldn't
But you see
True love doesn't part easily.
So now the pain stays
With the tears inside me
Where my heart used to be once.

Naïve Heart

My heart had decided that you were special
But my tears always knew you weren't.

Perfect Definition

We sang the same song together
But we were always out of sync.
A perfect definition of something
That was never meant to be.

Timing

You weren't for me
Nor was I for you.
I still believe our love was real
But if we were right for each other
The timing would have never been wrong.

– There's no such thing as 'wrong timing'

Amna Dhanani

Last Day of Love

On the last day of love
I knew what had happened,
What was happening
And what was going to happen.
Nothing about love
And its aftermath surprised me anymore.
I let the truth come to me
As a child comes to his mother
I accepted it the way it was.
I stopped wrapping my heart
With the sound of his voice
To comfort me
To let him stay after he was gone.
This time we both made the decision
To leave and stay gone
And I ripped off the band-aid
Letting the air heal my wounds
As it was supposed to.
I invited the hurt to take me
Because I knew
Healing only finds its way
When it's aware of the wound
Not when I'm hiding it inside my heart
Treasuring it like a reward.

Heartbreak

Even if there's no love anymore
Heartbreak still remains.

My Poetry

I wanted him to be my partner
He just wanted to be my poetry.

A Wish

I hope one day you'll fade away from my words
Just like you did from my life.

Belief in Love

My heart is broken
Not my love.
I will love again.

Numb

Is there anything fair in this world?
I'm too numb to feel happiness
But not numb enough to not feel pain.

Amna Dhanani

Hazy Memories

Sometimes my happy memories are so blur
I feel like I never lived them.

Mask

Thank God
For being able to put up a good front
Without it, our wounds would be on display
To be scratched with questions
We would never have the energy to answer.

– Mask, a false identity and a mandatory custom

Solitude

People drain me so much
What was feared in my life before
Is now much needed.

– *Solitude*

Death Sentence

Something that is time consuming
Is like a death sentence
To a mentally tired person.

Amna Dhanani

Fear

We are not always afraid of the dark
Sometimes it's the light that is scary
Sometimes not knowing
Seems like a better option
But it hardly is.

Realization

I looked back
And you looked at me.
In that moment I realized
We were never meant to be.

Differences

Do not loathe yourself
For not wanting
The same things as him.
Appreciate yourself
For knowing the difference
For knowing that you want him
But not what he wants.

– *You've come a long way*

Courage

After everything you've endured
It takes courage
To offer the kind of love you possess
And it takes the same amount of courage
To receive it.
If he doesn't have that
Then he doesn't deserve your love.

Self-acceptance

Don't worry
About how big the baggage you come with is
Since we all carry our own
We should accept ourselves with it
And if someone doesn't accept you as you are
It's their problem not yours.

Stood by Myself

When I looked into the mirror today, I realized
All these years I used to think that
Whenever I felt like giving up
You were the one to hold me together
But you see, in the end
You gave up on me
But I didn't give up on myself.

Stand Tall

So many times my heart has been broken
Sometimes even shattered into a million pieces
And broken yet again
Before it even got a chance to heal.
If it can still beat after all this
Then why won't I stand up
The way I'm supposed to
And let life lead me where I'm meant to be.

Fault

It's not your fault
If you fall for the wrong person
It is your fault when you don't get up.

Amna Dhanani

Rise

You became my fall
So I could become my rise.

Self-care

After a long time of wait and disappointments
My wounds began to heal themselves
Leaving some scratches behind
So I woke up one day
And kissed them better myself.

– Time cannot heal you without your efforts

Amna Dhanani

To be Okay

Sometimes we don't even realize
We have to allow ourselves to be okay.

Growing Apart

You slipped away from beneath my hands
Just like a river's flow.
I would never stop you from growing
Even if that meant we'd grow apart.

– I let you go

Amna Dhanani

Cleansed

I went into the river with you
And came out alone
I cleansed myself of your memories.

The Mistake

If our paths ever cross again
And we meet somewhere
Instead of turning away
I will greet you with a smile
As you were one of the best things
That happened to me
And then turn away
And leave you
Like the mistake you were, nonetheless.

Amna Dhanani

You Don't Belong Here

I built a home for you in my heart
And you broke it down.
So I built a home for you in my words
But now I'm the one throwing you out.

Moving On

Moving on from you
Was sweeter than
Falling in love with you.

Amna Dhanani

Self-love

I couldn't allow you to break me
You had already broken my heart
And that was enough.
So I unfolded myself
To refold into a new me
Whose every fragment now
Loves itself first.

Our End

Out of all the well-thought-out worst scenarios
I didn't think this would be our end.
We both fell out of love with each other
As the next chapter of our lives began.

Amna Dhanani

Happy Endings

Sometimes happy endings are not
What we thought they would be
But as long as you are happy
You shouldn't waste time wondering.

My Journey

My journey will always be incomplete
Until I find the kind of love
Which won't only stay
But will also be able to evolve with my love.
The kind of love
Which will be full of possibilities
And not a slave of this world
Out of helplessness.
Which won't only fulfill me
But it'll be capable of fulfilling our life together
As life unravels itself around us.
The kind of love
Which will have the potential to grow
Even if we reach a dead end
It won't give up looking for a way for us.
Its breath won't be dependent on time
But it'll end when time itself ends.

Self-acceptance introduced me to self-love
It made me realize
That love is the Soul of one's Existence
And love never leaves, people do.

– You used to be the Soul of my Existence

Words

Amna Dhanani

Wonders of Silence

I never thought someone's silence
Would fill my pen with words.

The Magic of Poetry

The verses may still fly
In the wind that slows down
Upon the arrival of love.

Poetry will be senseless
For those who do not heed
The words delivered by a dove.

The magic is created in the air
Where the clouds yearn to kiss
The blue skies above.

So read with your heart
Let the fire you hold within take over
Even in bleakness you might find love.

Amna Dhanani

Poetry is Incredible

A description of a poem can be a poem itself.

That's how incredible poetry is.

Embrace

Things got serious when
Instead of running away from my thoughts
I embraced them.

Amna Dhanani

My Darkest Thoughts

I never write down my darkest thoughts
I'm afraid they might find their way
To those who can relate to them
And what if those souls can't survive?
What I barely manage to survive
Every. Single. Day.

Fortitude

I want to live.
These four words are courage
In a world which brings me death
In different forms of pain each day.

Amna Dhanani

Twisted World

Don't deceive yourself by believing
That if you were able to write down
Whatever you're feeling
You will be magically healed.
It doesn't work that way
Sure, it sometimes helps to let things out
But sometimes the written truth will torture you
It'll be a reminder of the ugly reality
You had to deal with.
You'd think that penning your pain down
Would take it out of you
But words are just what you write
Whenever you read them
Your heart may turn cold or burn in agony
Because of how cruel your fate was to you.
You can't expect your writing
To make you feel better
But the act of writing
May give you some relief.

It's twisted isn't it?
Like everything else in this world.

– This is why sometimes I use my pain
To write about others' pain
So it won't come back at me

Pain

She expresses pain too well
Between her words
Which scream about the pain of this world
And yet there's no hint of her own hell at all.

Amna Dhanani

Old Journals

Whenever I find pain in my old journals
I caress my words
As if I'm comforting the young girl
Who had to endure so much
To make me who I am today.

The Irony

I don't write about you anymore
And that's my victory
But the irony is that I just lost to my victory.

Amna Dhanani

Healed Wounds

Sometimes I can only write about my wounds
When they are no longer there.

Be You

People will see
What they want to see in your words.
Just be true and just be you
That's all that matters.

Amna Dhanani

Art

When you're into art
Always remember
Not every piece is a masterpiece
But it is progress.
Every piece of yours is a piece of you
So don't belittle your work
Even if it's a small achievement
After a huge one.

Write For Yourself

Don't forget to write for yourself
From time to time
Even if it's something
That you can't share with others.

Amna Dhanani

Profound Moments

Poetry is capturing a feeling into words
Just as you capture a moment in a picture.

Freedom

The words that held me captive for years
Are the same words
Which have given me wings to fly today.

Thank you

How could I ever thank you for the respect,
acceptance, love, appreciation and support
you've shown to me and my words, going
through whatever I went through was worth it, if
it has helped even one soul. By allowing my
pain to speak to you, you've allowed my soul the
freedom to breathe peacefully. It has been a
privilege to share my pain and my healing with
you. Thank you for reaching another fragment of
my soul, I will be eternally grateful to you.

– Purpose fulfilled

About The Author

Amna Dhanani was 11 years old when she wrote something for the first time without being asked to. It was an article about mothers inspired by her mother. Subsequently, as she was praised for that article, she realized she could write and that's how her journey as a writer began, a journey in which she wishes to touch your soul with her words.

She has only studied till 8th grade in school. Since then, she has learned almost everything on her own, often with no help from others. Her keen observation of the world around her taught her a lot.

Amna Dhanani, also known for her debut poetry book My Existence Craves Yours is a diligent and a passionate writer from a small town in Sindh, Pakistan. She writes about her perception of the world, its love and beauty but also about its pain and suffering which causes heartbreak and teaches us the wisdom life demands for survival.

About The Book

You were the Soul to my Existence is a pure example of how the one you love is nothing else but the soul of one's existence and after it's gone, your life becomes lifeless, like leaves do in Autumn.

Amna Dhanani has continued the story from where she had left in her debut poetry book My Existence Craves Yours, giving every poem a special place in the flow once more, although You were the Soul to my Existence contains many different elements like heartbreaks of many kinds, traumatic childhood, infinite love in finite time, hardships, self-healing and growth.

When she was asked why there was only a slight hint about continuing the love story from her first poetry book instead of a clear mention, she said, both of her books are capable of standing alone, she didn't want them to rely on each other.

Please consider leaving a review on Amazon and
Goodreads.
A few words will help tremendously ♥